Wild Weather

Fabiola Sepulveda

Notes for the Grown-ups

This wordless book allows for a rich shared reading experience for children who do not yet know how to read words or who are beginning to learn. Children can look at the pages to gather information from what they see, and they can suggest text to tell the story.

To extend this reading experience, do one or more of the following:

Draw pictures of the things people wear in different types of weather.

Introduce vocabulary such as these words when looking at the pictures and telling the story you see:

- blizzard
- dry
- flood
- fog
- hail
- heat
- hurricane
- ice
- icicle
- lightning
- rain
- rainbow
- snow
- storm
- sun
- thunderstorm
- tornado
- wet

Talk together about the weather you are experiencing today. Also talk about extreme weather you have experienced and how you responded to it (for example, staying indoors).

After reading the pictures, come back to the book again and again. Rereading is an excellent tool for building literacy skills.

Watch video clips of different types of weather in action. Talk about what you see and hear.

Consultant

Cynthia Malo, M.A.Ed.

Publishing Credits

Rachelle Cracchiolo, M.S.Ed., *Publisher*
Emily R. Smith, M.A.Ed., *SVP of Content Development*
Véronique Bos, *VP of Creative*
Dona Herweck Rice, *Senior Content Manager*

Image Credits: all images from iStock and/or Shutterstock

Library of Congress Cataloging in Publication Control Number:
2024012455

TCM | Teacher Created Materials

5482 Argosy Avenue
Huntington Beach, CA 92649
www.tcmpub.com
ISBN 979-8-7659-6154-4
© 2025 Teacher Created Materials, Inc.
Printed by: 926. Printed in: Malaysia. PO#: PO11723